How To Get Answers Every Time you Pray.... About your Diet

Cleansing Your Temple

Chef Anna Nichole

Based on the original book, "How to Get Answers Every Time You Pray, The Power of Partnership"

©Copyright 2005 Dr. Ludie L. Hoffman

Revisions Created:

"HOW TO GET ANSWERS EVERYTIME YOU PRAY... About your Diet."

© Copyright 2021 Chef Anna "Nichole" Hoffman.

Interfaith University Press- All rights Reserved.

In partnership with AMC Consultants

It is not legal to reproduce, duplicate, or transmit any part of this document in either electronic means or printed format. Recording of this publication is strictly prohibited.

Acknowledgments

Thank you to Apostle Dr. Ludie L. Hoffman, my father, for allowing me the opportunity to revise and expound further on his original "How to Get Answers Every Time You Pray: The Power of Partnership © Copyright 2005" book. Dr. Ludie L. Hoffman has allowed me to share with you about how you can honor God by taking care of the body that He has given you. In this book, individuals will learn how to better care for their bodies, how to seek God in finding the right diet for them, how to trust God throughout their diet, and much more!

"How to Get Answers Every Time You Pray: About Your Diet", is a revision and has been expounded upon what has already been written and presented by Dr. Ludie L. Hoffman.

Table of Contents

What is a Diet?

"Do you not know that your body is the temple (the very sanctuary) of the Holy Spirit Who lives within you, whom you have received [as a Gift] from God? You are not your own, you were bought with a price purchased with a preciousness and paid for, [made His own]. So then, honor God and bring glory to Him in your body."

-1 Cor. 6:19-20

To diet comes from the Greek word **diaita**, which represents an overall concept of a healthy lifestyle including both mental and physical health, instead of a narrow weight-loss program.

Figuratively, the word means to withdraw from a specific course of food for a particular amount of time. I know what you are probably thinking, "Isn't dieting and fasting the same thing?" Let's compare these two terms to gain a greater knowledge of them...

To fast simply comes from an Old English root, **fæsten**, **"voluntary abstinence from food or drink, especially as a religious duty."**

Biblical fasting is simply the decision to refrain from substance for spiritual reasons. This term is discussed several times in the Bible. One primary example that demonstrates fasting being a regular occurrence is Matthew 6:16, where Jesus acknowledges His disciples, and He begins with, "When you fast," as opposed to "If you fast." In Matthew 9:15, Jesus also says "they will" [fast] about His followers – instead of "might".

Overall, the core difference between biblical fasting and abstaining from food as relation of a diet is the spiritual prospect of it. If you abstain from eating due to not having access to food, or attempting to lose weight, it's not viewed as biblical fasting – even if you are a religious person.

In short, biblical fasting and dieting both can be defined as abstaining from food – and sometimes other things – however, it all depends on the individual's reason for dieting. Many individuals decide to diet just to feel better about themselves, while others decide to diet to lose weight or due to specific health reasons. However, our overall purpose for dieting should be to show God that we will honor Him by taking care of the bodies He has created for us. God is trusting us to take care of our bodies, and it is our responsibility to dedicate them to Him.

Let's take one more look into 1 Corinthians 6:19-20, to assure that we grasp all that God has for us in this passage of scripture.

"Don't you realize that your body is the temple of the Holy Spirit, who lives in you and was given to you by God?."

This verse is a simple reminder that the Holy Spirit, God's Spirit, dwells within us. This verse is definitely an eye opener for believers to respect and take care of our bodies, as it should be. And then Paul writes, saying **"You do not belong to yourself, for God bought you with a high price. So, you must honor God with your body."**

Here, Paul enlightens us to remember that because our Savior Jesus Christ paid the crowning price – his life was sacrificed for us on the cross at Calvary – that we are eligible to be **partnered** with the Holy Spirit.

We are reminded in Isaiah of the cruel death that Jesus experienced for us...

"5 But he was wounded for our transgressions, he was bruised for our iniquities: the chastisement of our peace was upon him; and with his stripes we are healed.
6 All we like sheep have gone astray; we have turned everyone to his own way; and the Lord hath laid on him the iniquity of us all. 7 He was oppressed, and he was afflicted, yet he opened not his mouth: he is brought as a lamb to the slaughter, and as a sheep

before her shearers is dumb, so he openeth not his mouth.

-Isaiah 53:5-7

There are many instances that my motivation to care for my body wains. In cases like these, I often must remind myself about the 'high price' that Jesus paid for me with His life and how I have received his goodness. Oftentimes, I attempt to envision what it was like for Jesus to have been abused and arrested to the cross. To simply respect how out of submission and because He was in **partnership** with God, He was isolated from his Father for a period.

So, let me ask you. Has your motivation to care for your body waned? Do you desire extra force to receive a lifestyle or health-related behavior change? If so, imagine Jesus on the cross. Connect the dots concerning his affliction and the indwelling Spirit of God that is in you.

Never forget that he loves you so much that he willingly sacrificed his life for you. Rest with these truths. Accept them to encourage and prompt you to care for His temple, your body.

Prayer

Before we go any further let me give you a definition of the word *prayer* or *pray*. Pray as explained by Jesus means in the Greek **prosseuchomai** (pros-yoo-khom-ahee). The word is progressive starting with the noun ***euche***, which is a prayer to God that includes ***making a vow***.

The word expands to the verb ***euchomai***, a special term describing "an invocation, request or entreaty". Adding ***pros,*** in the direction of God, **prossechomai** becomes the most frequent word used for *prayer*.

Looking at meaning two here, Invocation, is where we will find the power of agreement. Remember in Genesis 11, the unity of the people caused God to take notice of what was going on at the Tower of Babel and come down to stop the work and confuse the languages. Translation- unity at work brings God's presence down!

Look at it from the positive. On the Day of Pentecost, they were all together with one accord and God came down again (Acts Chapter 2)!

Unity at work directed toward God for negative or positive will get God's attention. Now we have unity- that is if you have been born again, you have the measure of unity that brings you into the family of God. The key is to learn from the Word of God how to work that unity for the positive, productive reasons God gave it to you! Unity is not enough being left alone; it must be activated in the direction toward God!

IT!

Now let's deal with IT! One of the reasons many praying Christians have unanswered prayers is the IT! Some are praying for IT and IT does not come. Why? Because IT must be not only in unity with a person on Earth, but it must be loosed from heaven. The following process will get you anything you need (Philippians 4:19), want (Psalms 23), or desire from God (Psalms 37:4) concerning your diet; for it is the Father's good pleasure to give you the kingdom!

1. ***Analyze the situation-*** Find out what your desires are, what your debts are, what your sickness is, or what the fear is about. Find out how much of what it is you need to sustain yourself, your family, and the House of God!

2. 2 Corinthians 13:5 says that we must ask of God to help us to know ourselves, so we are not asking amiss!

3. ***Design-*** To be successful in your diet, we must first recognize that the Bible is our first and final authority. Because of this fact, then it is vital for us to understand that our bodies were designed to be healthy. Anything against that design will cause illness and disease. The first step to a successful diet is to admit God designed your body for greatness.

4. ***Desires-*** God has granted us desires, however, man has adjusted and confounded those desires for his own profit. Food is the prime example of this. ***God designed food*** to meet our desires and for teaching. However, man has taken God's designed foods and altered them to be addictive and monetized for his personal gain.

Therefore, we must line up our desires with God and put away man's way of doing things. When we do this, **we win this battle every time**.

5. ***Discipline-*** Oftentimes, I wonder why God did not design our bodies to only enjoy a certain number of calories daily and then allow our bodies to automatically stop us from eating. The reason being, God had a different plan for us, and He desires for us to seek Him in **all** things. That means the prime feared "D" word - despised more than **'DIET'** is ***Discipline***.

6. ***Daily-*** The main problem individuals have with healthy living is that it is a daily process! This simply means that each day we have a choice and must decide who we will serve, **God** or man? **God** or our desire for eating an

excessive amount of food? **God** or those decadent fudge brownies? Am I saying that we will never get to eat what we like? Not at all. You can have desserts, just remember they are a treat, not a meal.

Remember that daily you get to show God your love for Him by eating when you are hungry, stopping when your body is content (not your mind looking at the cake) and consuming less than you desired. Daily we win this battle, occasionally we lose.

It is the greatest absent attribute in our society today because advertisers do not desire for us to be disciplined. They want us impulsive, confounded and always in want. We must desire to be disciplined for our own good because no one can do it for us. Alongside discipline comes Godliness.

Eventually, it leads us to so much more of what God has in store for us. It is an essential step.

6. ***Diet-*** God has given us the absolute best of the best! Actual food hand-designed by our Creator cannot be compatible by anything man attempts to create. Eating foods in their natural form and getting as close as we can to God's **original** design; not allowing any food to position itself as an addiction is essential.
7. ***Desserts- "It is not good to eat too much honey, nor is it honorable to search out matters that are too deep." – Proverbs 25:27***

Here we see that even the Old Testament instructed us to go easy on the sugar! It is not a sin to consume honey (or sugar) in general, however, there are healthy limits to consuming, too. Portion control is far beyond just setting a bunch of rules that you never follow. They are boundaries to defend and guide us.

God knows our temptations, weaknesses, and our desires so we must put our Trust in Him, knowing that he has our best interest at heart. It is not His intention to steal joy from us with strict rules. He just simply knows what is best for us and wants to give us gentle and loving reminders to remain on that course.

Did you know that research has proven that the first few bites taste best? So, for example, let's say you are eating a decadent red velvet cake. The first few bites are going to taste amazing! After that, our taste buds weary, and it begins to taste less and less amazing with every forkful. The lesson? Have a bit of sugar. Slow down. Savor it, taste it, and enjoy it...just don't overdo-it!

8. Research God's Remedy- Just as you would ask your pharmacist or doctor which medication is best for a specific problem, ask the Great Physician to show you in His written Word what the cure is. Ask God for His perspective. Then search and research the Bible until you have allowed the Holy Spirit to convince you of the truth that Christ has redeemed you from the curse of the law (Galatians 3:13).

1. ***Ask, Seek, Knock***- Once you have gained an understanding of God's will according to scripture for yourself from the Word of God, then He hastens his Word to perform it (Matthew 7:7)! This simply means it consistently persists in growing intensity and faith until God hears your request and grants it! Keep praying and seeking God until you see the results that you want! Show God that you will put Him **first**, even in your diet! God gives us the desires of our hearts (Psalms 37:4), so

keep seeking Him (with your prayers) until the King of Heaven opens the door.

2. **Partner**- You may be saying "*...I ask, I seek, I knock, but I still can't seem to get my* breakthrough"! Then bring in the atomic bomb.... partners.... when it seems as though you have reached your faith limit- remember that there are other saints that have conquered this level of negative force and you have access to their faith through the power of agreement (James 5:14-16)! To fully see God's will manifest we must have other believers praying for us and with us concerning our eating habits and food addictions. It is extremely important to always surround yourself with individuals who have a heart for God, constantly praying and seeking God on your behalf. If you are wondering, "Why

does it seem like I persevere in this diet?" Maybe consider who you are surrounding yourself with. You can't surround yourself with individuals who never finish anything and expect different results. So, take a minute now and ask God to surround you with individuals who genuinely have a heart for God.

There have been many challenges in the past that I have faced and couldn't overcome until I partnered with other believers. Notice the Bible says, *"call for the Elders of the church"*. There are two principles here that should not be ignored:

1. *Elder*- means *older,* not necessarily in age, but maturity in the Lord! An elder is at least mature in the area that you are struggling with. **Warning**: if you have a struggle or challenge (such as a food addiction), a prayer partner with the same

challenge and/or struggle is not going to be able to build you up any further than where they are for, he has not developed himself to the point that he is strong enough to bear your infirmity and his! Therefore, instead of agreeing with God you begin to unite against God, and you get a Tower of Babel or a Tower of Confusion!

1. Remember that the binding and losing power is connected to the CHURCH. Make it a rule not to partner with anybody in prayer who is not firmly rooted in a local church! (At least not to get your deliverance!) We cannot change our diet alone; God places specific individuals in our lives to keep us rooted in Him. To be successful in our diet we need strength, strength from God and strength from

other believers. It is fine to pray with a person who is not in church who understands that the focus of the prayer is for their edification mainly, but remember if you need strength, you must find strong prayer partners (Matthew 18:18-19). You may go as far as to say that you already have a prayer partner, but there is still a problem. In such a case, start at steps 1-4 and if all lines are clear, bring in another prayer partner and another and another until you have enough power in prayer to bind the strong man or negative force that is blocking your flow of blessing! Just make sure every prayer partner understands and has done the above things and can agree with you that this IT is the will of God, and he wants you to have IT. Start building your prayer partnership today!

9. Praise and worship God in Faith and watch it manifest!

10. Separate from bad company, negative friends, bad teaching and preaching not in faith in God's total Word (I Corinthians 15:33).

11. If the enemy attacks you with doubt- do it again (Galatians 6:6).

The bottom line is to reach you overall goals through your diet you must line up with your prayer partner's level of faith and the will of the Father in Heaven. Well, how do we know the will of the Father concerning our diet? We must know, agree, and pray according to the Word of Almighty God. If God says to d**I**e**T**, bank on that d**I**e**T**, agree with God! Say what God says and you will truly have whatsoever you say! Now how do you know what your **dIeT** is? Matthew 6:33 deals with seeking first righteousness and He will commence to dropping it on you!! How do you seek the kingdom?

1.) **Watch and pray for opportunities to sow-** finance, time, energy, and prayer into an anointed ministry that is spreading the Good News of THE KINGDOM OF GOD! A ministry with VISION.

2.) **Preach the Word**- Witness to friends and neighbors. Share your Testimony! Share how God delivered you from your food addiction and/or how God lead you through your diet. Give away tracts, good sound Christian books, tapes, and videos. Get the gospel out any way you can in the Spirit of God. (Pray about it!!)

3.) **Put God first**- Stop thinking of how much you can get from God and think about how much you can do for God's kingdom! You may only desire a few groceries for yourself, but the kingdom of God may call for you to have an entire food pantry to assist other people. Pray until you find out what God wants you to have because *that* is your need. Seek first the kingdom and His righteousness!

Start helping others in their time of need, and God will Bless you in return! Am I saying that you should just run off and sow financial seed to everything asking and moving or looking like the kingdom? No!! Would you sow peas one or two or three to a field? No!! Because you would have to go to two or three different locations just to get started on a pot!! The bottom line is to sow where:

4. God leads,

5. The ground is good,

6. The Gospel is being preached,

7. Souls are being saved, and

8. Christians are edified.

Do all of this under the anointing or the witness of the Holy Spirit! Pray. God will direct your journey including your dieting journey. What is ***IT***? Let's touch and agree and it is done according to God's will.

God's Will

We have already established that God's Word is his will. But let's dig deeper!! If you genuinely want to be blessed, you must allow God to speak to your heart about your diet and learn how to back it up with scripture. You must make that scripture and revealed Word from God your faith. That's right, the moment God makes a word alive in your spirit you have faith. *Now*! Hebrews 11:1 says, "*Now faith is the substance of things hoped for, the evidence of things not seen.*"

Romans 10:17 tells us, *faith comes by hearing and hearing by the Word of God.*

The Diet from God

It is important that we consult God in ALL that we do, even in our diets. There is a covenant from the scriptures that I want to share with you...

In the Bible, there was a Covenant between Daniel and God. The Jewish noble Daniel and his followers are taken by the Babylonians and initiated into the company of the Babylonian King Nebuchadnezzar. The Babylonians attempt to serve Daniel and his men rich food ("the King's meat" and wine), but Daniel was careful of God's law of "unclean foods." Daniel 1:8 states: "***But Daniel made up his mind that he would not defile (taint, dishonor) himself with the king's finest food or with the wine which the king drank; so, he asked the commander of the officials***

that he might [be excused so that he would] not defile himself."

Daniel stated that he and his followers would only consume a **diet** of only vegetables ("pulse"). After 10 days, they became healthier and stronger than the Babylonians, and his **diet** became a partial presentment of his action to the King's authority.

I enjoy reading the story of Daniel because it encourages me to resist the harmful influences of the outside world. Daniel's story has impacted Believers all over the world to demonstrate their love for God by dieting. Many Believers have taken it upon themselves to take the "diet" aspect of Daniel's story literally. Simply encouraged by faith and fitness, many Christians around the world, like Daniel, occasionally restricting themselves to only eating fruits and vegetables for a 21-day process.

Daniel's decision to not eat the King's food simply demonstrates a basic component of authentic integrity and the uncompromising life: you must draw lines where Scripture draws them. If the actuality of God's Word contends the world's wisdom on a specific issue, you must align yourself with God's Word. As believers, we must consult God, trusting that He will lead us and show us which diet is best for us.

The Challenge

I want to simply challenge you for 14 days to seek God concerning your diet. Whether your diet is for weight loss, weight-gain, or even just for a healthier temple; I want you to keep knocking on His door until he opens. This will allow God to provide you with His guidance, support, and love on your journey. Dieting isn't a quick fix, but it does have lasting change!

The lasting change is an adjustment in our thinking, in our actions, and in our hearts and minds.

As Christians, we believe that God is the source of all life. Through Him, we find our true selves and full health. When it comes to dieting, we often either work on it alone or simply pray the pounds away. Both are extremes. I believe that God is looking to meet us in the middle and join us on our journey equipping us through His power, strength, wisdom, and love. And that is what this Challenge is all about, it is a little jump start for you to fuse your relationship with God and your dieting ambitions.

In all areas of life, God is Lord of it all, if we only offer and abide. It takes an active role on our part to return to God over and over and connect to Him. For it is us who wanders away so quickly and frequently. God never leaves us, but we must attune our minds and hearts to He who is with us always, or we end up just walking in our own strength and power-which doesn't accomplish much.

If you want to lose weight and stick to a diet you must start from a humble place of honesty.

There are some foundational questions you have to ask yourself and most importantly, you have to be completely truthful (with yourself and with God).

When it comes to your diet, no one really knows all of the choices you make, that is ultimately between you and the Lord and anyone else you would like to share it with.

In order for you to succeed, you have to be honest throughout the entire journey, and if you aren't sure about and if there's something you're unaware of that's holding you back. I encourage you to pray about it, because truth is the start of a diet you will stick to.

You will have the opportunity to ask and answer these key questions in just a bit, but before we jump into that let's talk about the number one reason people give up on their dieting goals and things you can do to avoid this.

It is so easy to say, *"oh, I have dieted so many times before and struggled to lose weight and keep the weight off."*

Or, *"I was successful for a while and then got back into bad eating habits"* and start to doubt your future attempts.

Overall, the *number one reason* I often see from many individuals for quitting is that they fail to give themselves credit for their success.

You must be mindful of this trap. Any positive change you make is a victory!

Even if you haven't lost any weight so far or think you haven't made enough progress here are some things to look for and feel good about along the way.

Important Questions to ask yourself

I want you to be prepared to take the first step.

There will be temptations you may have to face but having the right kind of thinking will really help you to overcome any dieting obstacle.

First, I recommend **using a notebook and some note cards** that are specifically for your diet journey.

Then, write down three separate questions in your notebook.

1. Do you Truly Desire Change

Do you really want to be healthy?

Do you really want to lose weight?

The very first step is answering this to yourself honestly.

Do you really, truly desire change in your life?

If you really desire to change and believe that this is what the Lord would have for you to do, write down in your notebook, *"I dedicate my body to God, believing and receiving the total manifestation of change."*

This is a powerful declaration!

The **Lord will help you with any struggle** you have, anything that keeps us from him or doing his will.

We will never be alone.

However, he also **gives us the tools we need to succeed** and we must be the ones to take action.

It has to be you.

You are the only one who can take action in your health journey.

This first question is so important because if you are not truly ready, it will be much easier for temptations and setbacks to get the best of you.

God want us to be healthy and experience full joy! We need to be healthy to be able to share the gospel, help others and step into the roles we were meant to glorify God.

Sticking to a diet can be challenging, but if you ask yourself why you will find your motivation. When you document your progress, you will become so much more involved with the process.

Eventually, you will be on your way to overcoming emotional eating, binge eating, and similar setbacks that get on your way to achieving health! When we learn to be satisfied and do all things for the glory of God. We have happier, healthier lives just the way God intended.

Scriptures to Encourage

-1 Cor. 6:19-20

"Do you not know that your body is the temple (the very sanctuary) of the Holy Spirit Who lives within you, whom you have received [as a Gift] from God? You are not your own, you were bought with a price purchased with a preciousness and paid for, [made His own]. So then, honor God and bring glory to Him in your body."

-Romans 12:1

> *"I beseech you therefore, brethren, by the mercies of God, that you present your bodies a living sacrifice, holy, acceptable to God, which is your reasonable service."*

-Philippians 4:1

"Therefore, my beloved and longed-for brethren, my joy and crown, so stand fast in the Lord, beloved."

-Philippians 4:13

"I can do all things through Christ who strengthens me."

-1 Corinthians 10:31

"Therefore, whether you eat or drink, or whatever you do, do all to the glory of God."

-Hebrews 12:11

"For the moment all discipline seems painful rather than pleasant, but later it yields the peaceful fruit of righteousness to those who have been trained by it."

-Psalm 145:15-16

"The eyes of all looks to you in hope; you give them their food as they need it. When you open your hand, you satisfy the hunger and thirst of every living thing."

-Isaiah 55:1-2

"Is anyone thirsty? Come and drink even if you have no money! Take your choice of wine or milk-it's all free! Why spend your money on food that does not give you strength? Why pay for food that does you no good? Listen and I will tell you where to get food that is good for the soul!"

-Colossians 3:2

"Think about the things of heaven, not the things of earth."

-Lamentations 2:22-23

"The steadfast love of the Lord never ceases; his mercies never come to an end; they are new every morning; great is your faithfulness."

-Nehemiah 8:10

"Do not sorrow, for the joy of the Lord is your strength".

A Prayer for Complete, Good Health

Heavenly Father,

We praise You for this day, and every day that we get to wake up. Each day is laced with purpose, and we ask for Your wisdom and guidance. Help us to live each day well, and for Your glory, from start to finish.

Thank You for Your Word, which breathes life into our souls and minds. You promise to meet us there, in study and in prayer. Thank You for the sacrifice, Jesus made on the cross, paying with His life for our ease of access to our Heavenly Father through prayer and Scripture.

Father, you remind us throughout Scripture that You are faithful to Your people.

Jeremiah 33:6 says, "Nevertheless, I will bring health and healing to it; I will heal my people and will let them enjoy abundant peace and security." So often, as in the Old Testament, we rebel, neglect to care for ourselves as You do, and end up tired and sick. But Father You are faithful to enwrap us in Your healing love each time we turn back to You.

Forgive us for neglecting to care for the life You have entrusted us with. The life that You have purposed specifically to do more than we can ask for or imagine. When we go our own way, we wear ourselves down, physically, and mentally. Other times, we train physically but neglect other things. Father, strengthen us to obtain the joy You bless us with. Help us to walk freely in Your love.

For as Paul reminds us in 1 Timothy 4:8, "Although training your body has certain payoffs, godliness benefits all things--

holding promise for life here and now and promise for the life that is coming." Send us more of Your Holy Spirit, to help us focus on Your Word daily. Give us hearts like Jesus.

Give us the wisdom to seek You first each day before each decision. It's often the little thoughts and daily decisions that lead us into a sudden spiral of bad health. Enlighten us and guide us through Your Word. Let our hearts desire more of You each day. In Jesus Name. Amen!

A Prayer to control eating habits

Lord, I pray that you will give me the strength to resist the desires I have for unhealthy eating habits. Lord I ask that you replace those desires with the will to live and eat healthy. Please help me not use food as a comfort. I pray that I find comfort in you when I am tempted to indulge in things I shouldn't eat. I choose to be healthy mentally, physically, and spiritually for your glory.

Father, we praise You for blessing us with proper nutrition. From the first spark of humanity, you provided perfectly for us. In the desert, you fed Your people. ***"Miraculously, each person and each family—regardless of how much they gathered—had exactly what they needed."*** *(Exodus 16:18)*

Thank You for sending Jesus to earth! He understands the temptation of food for he was tempted by the devil in the desert while starving.

There are so many that are starving, too hungry to taste food as they focus on surviving each day. Uphold their spirits as they wait on You, Lord, for Your perfect provision. Comfort their hearts and strengthen them. Help us to trust You and be to be ready and willing to help when and how we can.

Each beautiful person was created with perfect intent. **"For You shaped me, inside and out."** (Psalm 139:13) Individuality cannot be categorized, yet we seek to... and it pushes many of us in front of the mirror in despair. You made each person beautifully, despite the imperfections of humanity. The food You provide was never meant to be used as a tool to wield hatred towards any body type. Forgive the grasp of control we continually attempt to grip by calculating our diets for immoral reasons.

From gluttony and overindulgence to self-starvation and vanity, we confess that our focus on food is often misguided. Forgive our failure to let go and let You show us what is good and right to include in our diets.

Guide our eating habits and protect us from additives that intend to harm and hook us.

Father, we know that the only way to make peace with food is to lean on You.

"You direct me on a path that leads to a beautiful life. As I walk with You, the pleasures are never-ending, and I know true joy and contentment" (Acts 2:28) We pray the active and living truth of this verse over our lives today, and always. In Jesus' Name, Amen.

A Prayer of Joy

Heavenly Father, how I bless and thank You for the glad tidings of great joy that were given to all people. Thank You for Jesus, and the joy and peace that floods the hearts of all who have believed in Him, the rock of their Salvation.

Lord, I praise and magnify Your glorious name for all Your goodness and love towards me, and to all who are called by Your name, for in You is the fullness of joy.

Help me to share this joy of knowing Jesus with all those who You place in my path, and I pray that throughout the world there may be many sinners today who are saved by grace through faith in the shed blood of Christ Jesus, so that they too may experience the joy which is freely available to all who believe in the gospel of grace. "O Father in heaven, I ask that you gladden and refresh my spirit. Purify my heart and mind so that I may be at one with you. Even when I am beset by troubles and despair, guide me toward your light and be my refuge. Through you, I no longer feel sorrow or grief. In your love, I can rejoice in everlasting happiness and joy. I will place my anxieties at your feet in the knowledge that you gave me each struggle so that I may triumph and learn. I confess and believe that I have received the joy of the Lord in Jesus' name. Amen!"

Understanding Redemption

God is able to establish us in the faith according to the plan of redemption which had been hidden over the ages. After the Fall in the Garden of Eden, God spoke and outlined the plan. What He laid down put Satan out of business completely. Praise God! He has commanded that the plan of redemption be revealed to His people by His Word. This outline will help you, step by step, understand the reality of it and prevent Satan from lording over you.

3. **The Plan of Redemption called for an Incarnation** (The Union of Divinity with Humanity in Jesus Christ).

Man was the key figure in the Fall. Therefore, it took a man, Jesus, to be the key figure in the redemption of man. When we were born into this world, ruled by Satan, we did not naturally know God. Therefore, the objective of the incarnation is that men may be given the right to become sons of God by receiving the nature of God (John 1:12-13; II Peter 1:3-4).

3. **Redemption Comes from Knowledge.**

God's divine power has already provided everything that pertains to life and godliness. You can escape from the corruption in the world and partake of the divine nature of God. And you can have peace and grace multiplied to you through the knowledge of God and of Jesus our Lord (I Peter 1:1-4). It's there for you! But this revelation knowledge is not sense knowledge, doctrine, philosophies, and creeds. It is the reality and full truth of the Word of God revealed by the Holy Spirit (James 3:13-18). Revelation knowledge is literally knowledge brought to you by revelation!

3. **Satan's Lordship Has Been Broken.**

Revelation 12:11 tells us that the believers overcome by the blood of the lamb and by

the word of their testimony, or confession. Confession brings possession. Boldly confess, *"I am an overcomer by the blood of the Lamb and by the word of my testimony. I am redeemed from the lordship of Satan. I can stop his assignments every time."* (II Corinthians 10:4; James 4:7). Satan is not the head of the Church. Jesus is the Head of the Church (Ephesians 4:15-16, 5:23; Colossians 1:18, 2:10). Satan has no rule over you. Hallelujah!

4. **You Are Bought With A Price.**

I Corinthians 6:19-20 tells us we are the temple of the Holy Spirit, which is received from God. This means that we don't own ourselves. We were bought with a price paid through the plan of redemption. Because of that, we should glorify God in our bodies and spirits.

9. **God's Response.**

When you begin to take your place and assume your rights and privileges in Christ, then God begins to respond to you. The Word gives us our inheritance (Acts 20:32; Colossians 1:12). As you study the scriptures in this outline, our prayer is that you come to the full knowledge of who you are in Christ, especially considering the redemption plan. God will bless you! Amen!

Understanding Confession

Words are spiritual, they carry power. The words we speak are of vital importance to our lives. Jesus said, *"I say unto you, that every idle word those men shall speak, they shall give account thereof in the day of judgment. For by thy words thou shalt be justified, and by thy words thou shalt be condemned"* (Matthew 12:36-37).

When God created the human race, he placed in us the special ability to choose our own words and speak to them forth at will. That ability makes the human being different from all other creatures, even the angels. Angels can speak but they can only speak the words God tells them to speak. They act, but only by the command of God.

Man's unique ability to choose and speak words has become a key factor in the development of humanity.

Proverbs 12:14 tells us that we shall be satisfied with good by the fruit of our mouths. In Matthew 12:34, Jesus said, *"...out of the abundance of the heart the mouth speaketh."*

If we are not enjoying the reality of God's Word, it is because our confession has us bound. Confession of the Word of God isn't lying, for what we must realize is that we are not trying to get God to do anything. The benefits God has given us in His Word are ours already and Satan is trying to steal them!

So, confessing isn't lying. It's a statement of truth. If you didn't know Jesus bore your sickness and disease and told someone you were healed because of your own merits, then you would be lying. But to tell someone that you are healed because the Bible says, *"by His stripes you were healed,"* is speaking the truth that Jesus has already redeemed you from the curse of the law (Deuteronomy 28; Galatians 3:13).

Here are five basic confessions for you to use so that you can enjoy all that God has for you:

1. **Jesus is My Lord.** Philippians 2:9-11

"I confess the complete lordship of Jesus Christ. Jesus is Lord overall and He has given me authority. As I confess Him, His Word and His Name, and resist Satan in His Name, Satan must bow His knee."

2. **I Do Not Have a Care.** I Peter 5:7; Psalms 37:23-24

"I cast all my care on Jesus because He cares for me. He upholds me as He guides my steps."

3. **I Do Not Want.** Psalms 23:1; Philippians 4:19

"The Lord is my Shepherd. I shall not want. For my God supplies all my need according to His riches in glory by Christ Jesus.

4. **I Am Free from Sin, Sickness, Sorrow, Grief and Fear.** Isaiah 53:3-5; Matthew

8:17; I Peter 2:24

"Every sin, sickness, disease, sorrow and grief were laid on Jesus so that I could be free from them. Therefore, today I

am forgiven, healed, healthy and well. I live in divine health."

5. **Jesus is made unto me Wisdom, Righteousness, Sanctification and Redemption.**

I Corinthians 1:30; Colossians 2:10

"I confess that Jesus is my wisdom, righteousness, sanctification, and redemption. Only in Him am I entirely complete."

Continue to change your circumstances by filling your heart with the Word of God. Confess these truths and other scriptures so that the words that come out of your mouth are life-changing words. Let your word be God's word!

YOUR OPPORTUNITY TO PARTNER

We are seeing that partnership is indeed dynamic. But partnership is not a one-sided relationship. As the Apostle Paul said, "*I thank my God upon every remembrance of you... For your fellowship in the gospel from the first day until now... because I have you in my heart; since both in my bonds, and in the defense and confirmation of the gospel, ye are all partakers of my grac*e (Philippians 1:3, 5,7)." Paul was saying "I have you in my heart, I'm praying for you and I'm not going to let you fail!" His partners had become a major part of his ministry. They fought alongside him in prayer, they ministered to his needs, and provided for other ministers that he sent to help build them spiritually. That's how partnership works.

The Partners have a significant role in this ministry. God provides for the ministry through them- through their prayers, words of encouragement and support, and through their giving to what God is doing through the ministry. And every day we see and hear of the great rewards they are receiving because of their partnership. If God is directing you to become a Partner, or if you are already a Partner, press in to get a revelation of God's will for you, and then get ready for the adventure and rewards that come when you release the power of partnership in your life.

The Blessing of the Twice Sown Seed

"And he...took the five loaves, and two fishes, and looking up toward heaven he blessed, and brake, and gave the loaves to his disciples, and the disciples to the multitude. And they did all eat, and were filled: and they took up of the fragments that remained twelve baskets full. And they that had eaten were about five thousand men beside women and children" (Matthew 14:19-21).

Sowing into "How to get Answers Every time you Pray....About your Diet" stretches further than the hundreds of lives "How to get Answers Every time you Pray... About your Diet" touches. It stretches from orphanages to healing ministries to evangelical meetings to medical teams. We reach all over the globe through the principle of the twice sown seed.

When you give to "How to get Answers Every time you Pray.... About your Diet", a portion of every gift is given to other ministries that reach people we can't. We re-sow a portion of your gift and product purchase into lives all over the world. And just like the boy who gave his loaves and fish to Jesus, we see the increase on the seed-faith gifts of our partners. Through partnership in ministry, we are reaching greater numbers of people than any of us could reach on our own- people who have no other way to hear the good news.

We stand with ministries which train and minister through educating, credentialing, and assisting men and women in the Word of God, prayer, and divine leadership. We support outreaches which conduct yearly ministerial conference in several countries, providing Bibles in English and other native languages to equip Pastors to win the lost to Christ...a tremendous need! Providing theological training and books for Pastors and ministers, developing Bible schools, helping the children, feeding the poor, promoting soul winning and reaching the lost and church planting. We promote the gospel through broadcasting Gospel and Christian music as well as local, national, and international ministers on www.WVIURadio.net. We give into other ministries that teach local ministers by the hundreds every year in Guatemala, send evangelistic teams into the isolated Islands and mountains of the Philippines, and telecast the good news across Eastern Europe.

Orphan children in Haiti, former gang members in Los Angeles, Bible school students in Italy and troubled girls in Tennessee are all among the millions of lives touched by the love of our partners giving.

In addition, we support locally with our children's ministries, volunteer services programs, campus and young adult outreach, medical assistance, job creation, evangelism, continuing education assistance, clothing, food, teaching and preaching.

You enable us to put legs to our prayers by putting substance into our hands to be effective soldiers of the cross. As a result, you will share the reward of this harvest someday! Lives are changed Eternally. Blessings overflow to the giver. That's the power of partnership. That's the power of the twice-sown-seed!

"How to get Answers Every time you Pray.... About your Diet" Ministries

A PARTNER...........

One who shares responsibility in some common activity with another individual or group.

Our Part is to...

Pray daily that God's Blessing be
upon you Study and diligently seek
the Word of God

Minister to you monthly in a teaching letter

Furnish a partnership package with Certificate, Partner card and Book

Offer from time to time, a special gift for your spiritual edification and growth.

Your Part is to...

Pray for us always

Support meetings in your area

Sow financially into this ministry as the Lord shall direct

Always uplift the ministry, the minister(s), and their family with the words you speak.

"Chef Anna Nichole, I want to access the Power of this anointed Prayer Partnership!"

My Name is:

____

My Address is:

____

Phone: ___________________________

Age: __________ M _____ F _____

I am writing my prayer request on this form.

Enclosed is my love gift of $

_______________________________________.

I am pledging __ $7 __$10 __$20 __$100 __$500 __Other

$____ per month to

help you accomplish the vision of winning the lost and encouraging the saints through the Word of God!

_______________________________________, **Signature**

Prayer

Request____

____

____

____

____

____

PRAYER FOR MINISTRY PARTNERS

Father, in the Name of Jesus, we pray to you on behalf of our all our partners, who pray for us, support our local meetings, sow financially into this ministry, and always uplift the ministry, our minister(s) and their family with the words that they speak.

Father, we thank you for our partners and for their service and dedication to serve you. Thank you that they bring forth the fruit of the Spirit: love, joy, peace, long-suffering, gentleness, goodness, faith, meekness, and temperance.

Father, thank you that our partners are good ground, that they hear Your Word and understand it, and that the Word bears fruit in their lives. They are like trees planted by rivers of water that bring forth fruit in its season. Their leaf shall not wither, and whatever they do shall prosper.

From the first day we heard of our partners, we have not stopped praying for them, asking God to give them wise minds and spirits attuned to his will, and so acquire a thorough understanding of the ways in which God works. Our partners are merciful as our Father is merciful. They will judge only as they want to be judged. They do not condemn, and they are not condemned. Our partners forgive others and people forgive them. They give and men will give to them- yes, good measure, pressed down, shaken together, running over will they pour into their laps for whatever measure they us with other people, they will use in their dealings with them.

Father, we ask you to bless our partners with all spiritual blessings in heavenly places that good will might come to them. They are generous and lend freely. They conduct their affairs with justice. Lord, Your Word says that surely, they will never be shaken.

They are righteous men and women who will be remembered forever. They will have no fear of bad news; their hearts are steadfast, trusting in you.

Lord, we ask that your plans be fulfilled in their lives, and we thank you for your mercies on their behalf. In Jesus' name we pray. Amen.

Colossians 1:9 Psalm 112:5-9 Jeremiah 29:11

About The Author

Anna Nichole Hoffman, known professionally as *Chef* Anna Nichole, graduated high school at the age of 15. She immediately enrolled in her local college to begin her culinary career, where she studied culinary arts for 3 years.

She obtained professional skills in her field and training from some of the most honored chefs in her city. Anna has always had a passion to serve others through cooking. At the age of 5, Anna knew that she wanted to become a chef, she shared this passion for cooking with her family. Throughout the years, God has increased her passion to not only cook, but to also serve others through the great mission. She volunteers with a wide range of non-profits and outreaches to feed the homeless and those in need.

Made in the USA
Columbia, SC
16 April 2025

56678393R10043